21 Years and Going

Mr. Strong

B. Dey

Introduction

I was always mad in the world I lived in. I always knew that I was adopted, when I was a young boy. My childhood was not the best for me, and it really hit my heart hard. This happening to a young boy, is not a good thing to experience but I went through it. I been through so many foster homes, I would had thought I had five moms and five dads. The people who I stayed with did not treat me right or wanted me to be with them. I really did not like to be in the foster homes. Then, I went from so many foster homes I thought something was wrong with me because if my own parents do not want me then who will. I started to get a big trust issue, because people told me they wanted me, but then lie and gave me away.

As time moved on I did not want to trust anyone. As a result, it leads to a lot of people getting hurt that was in my life. I do not want to leave out that I did have one little sis name Odessa, and a little brother named Justin, which are both blood to me. I did have some positive to my life. Therefore, while you read more of my book, I hope you do not think this book is just me telling sob stories, but more of lessons, feelings, and some great things that came from me being adopted.

Jumping Bean

One day my siblings and I was told that we were going to a home to stay with a nice husband and wife. I figured out that most time when they said nice husband and wife that meant they were an ok couple. This is the start of many lies I went through. As a kid, you did not think adults would be so uncaring, but most are. I was so happy to have a mom and dad to call my own. When you are a child, you just want to be loved and cared for.

The last thing on your mind is that the mom and dad that you are with do not want you. Then, after two weeks went by I see a group of people coming to pick me and my siblings up from the house we was staying at and dropping us off at another family. At this point, I am confused, but I do not worry because I am a child that does not really know anything.

This family had already kids of their own, and once I got there, it was as if they had too many kids in the house because they treated me as if I was not even there. I hated every minute being there, so one way I tried to get attention was to cry. I do not think that worked, because they still did not come to me. However, I think it did make the parents not want me and my brother and sister.

As a result, we were on the move again. This was now the third house, and I started to see a pattern and felt some type of way. I started to think to myself and ask myself is there something wrong with me. At my age I should never have those type of thoughts. I should be thinking about how I could get a lot of mud on my clothes when I am outside having fun. In addition, I really started to get mad and did not want to trust any parents I went to, because all they do is, give me up to another family.

Which I was right, because after another 2 weeks went by I was on the road again. I believe that every house I went to I never took my clothes out of my black trash bags, because I knew I was going to another house in two weeks. I started not caring for the parents and crying so much. I knew I was getting on the parents nerves, because they use to yell at me. I knew they did not want to deal with me, because I remember one day they was leaving to go get some food. My brother and sister got in the car and I could not find my shoes. The parents drove off without me in the car and locked the door with me inside all alone. I was so mad so I started to cry so much, and they did not even feed me that day.

The days of being there was so horrible that I was counting the days for two weeks to come around, because I knew my brother, sister, and I would be leaving again. That day came so much slower, then being with the other three families. I think I was so happy to leave that home even though; really, inside I was sad again that we were moving again from this home.

Arriving at the next home there was an old grand ma that had many kids she was watching over and I was just one of the many mouths she had to feed now. I remember it was so many kids in the house, which we all slept on a big bed. This was the first house that I been to that if I cried the grand ma would come over and tell me to stop crying but I would still do it, and then she would make me do some chores. I really did not like to do chores. I never really liked to clean anything even at the age I am at right now I am lazy at cleaning.

This house also had given my siblings and me a godmother that we could see every Saturday. I guess the government thought we needed something positive in our lives so we can feel better about are situation. It did work for a little, because are godmother use to give us candy, and we use to play so many fun games. She was the best ever, and we loved her. One day when we were supposed to see her, but we founded out that she died. It was one of the worst days I would ever had. She was everything to use, and losing her was like losing part of our hearts.

Then, we got more bad news me and my siblings found out that we had to move again, but this time to a bigger building with bunk beds and a lot of kids that was in the same situation we was in. At this point I just told myself that I am no good for any family, and nobody was going to change my mindset.

The BIG Surprise

It all started on a normal day for me where I was at the foster home with several other male and female kids, who was waiting for that day to be adopted. The normal day that I had there was playing with other kids and my siblings. The worst feeling I had to experience there was seeing couples come through and thinking they would adopt me, but going on to the other kids. The couples never looked my way.

I was not the sweetest kid there, because of what I been through. In addition, no one wanted to have 3 kids, because I had a brother and sister that was my everything. I was like a package deal; if you adopted me then it was as if they had to take my sister and brother.

Then, one day a surprise came a couple came in and was looking for three young kids. The couple told the foster home leader, that they wanted to change three little kids lives, and do not care how messed up the kids history is. The couple started to walk around and when they saw my siblings and me, they just knew they had to take us. They wanted to get to know us first, so they told us they would come twice a month to take us out to eat and have fun. I thought it was all a joke. They came back next week and we had a great time, but after they dropped us off, I told myself that they would not come back.

I still had the mindset that everyone would tell me a lie and I always guarded my heart. Then one day something big happened in my life the couple came back I was bewildered. Then weeks and months went by and they keep on coming my hearted started to change, but not all the way. Then that big surprise came where the couple told us that were we ready to go home for good. I was happy but still somewhat mad, because I did not want to go to another home, and then leave after 2 weeks.

They truly loved us, because after two weeks, they still keep us, and I was so happy to be a Dyer. That was the day that my new parents were Garrett, and Julie Dyer.

New Home

Being in a new home and having my own room to my self was so different. I still was guarding my heart, because I still really did not know a lot about these parents. They gave me everything I want and I was so happy for once in my life, but even still I had in my thoughts that this was too true to be real.

I was so quiet and just played with my siblings a little. I use to have nightmares about my mom, and just everything that happen to me in my past. The Dyers tried to get me to talk, but I did not speak. I did do a lot of crying, because when I did not get my way I would cry. However, they did something that helped me become a better kid and not spoil me rotten, because after a while if no one came I would stop crying.

First Christmas

Christmas was never big for me, because the families I was with did not give me anything or made that day a big deal. Therefore, when Christmas came around when I was in my new home, my eyes got big. I saw so many presents for my siblings and me.

I was opening the presents so fast, that my parents were like you can slow down. I was full of joy. They even made a big breakfast, and then later on that day, the Dyers family came over and had dinner. I meet so many of my new cousins, uncles, and aunts it was fun, because many of my cousins were my age so it was fun to play with other kids.

At the end of the day, I went to bed, so happy and my heart start to warm up. My guard started to go down, because I felt loved from the new family. Right before I went to sleep the Dyers came in to tuck me in my bed; they said that they loved me. I never heard that word come from a parent, so it was strange, but I loved to hear it.

Bad kid

I remember I use to be bad in school, when I was younger. I use to get in fights and I never really got good grades.

When I first got into school I still was not talking, and I did not have any friends. They had to put me in a small class with three other kids so I can learn better. I did most of my work in that room and I had a speech problem, so I did not know how to say some letters. My parents even tried to pay someone to teach me on more of how to succeed in school.

I then had times in school where I fought this one kid, because I was so passionate about a lot of stuff, because of my history. It all started when this kid told me that my mother was a b-word. I started to fight the kid, and then the teacher broke us up. This was when I was in elementary school. I was suspended for couple of days, and I told my parents why I fought. The funny thing was after a week went by me and the kid I fought became friends, because we were young and did not know much.

I did other things in elementary school that I would not be proud of, so after I was done in elementary school my parents sent me to a private school. They did this so I could do better in school, and stay away from fighting people, and distractions. They were right for doing this, but what they did not know at the time that I would get in more fights.

The school I went to was called Archbishop Neale School (ANS) and it was like 90 percent Caucasian and 10 percent African American. I did not want to go to this school, because most of the new friends I made at my elementary school were going to a public middle school. I was always mad, because people started to mess with me, because I was black calling me names. I told my parents and they did not believe me, because at the time I use to lie a lot, but this time I was telling the truth.

One day on the playground, this one kid was trying to make me mad by saying mean things and saying how ugly I was and started to push me. My parents told me not to get in any fights, or I will be going to a private high school. I already hated going to a private middle school so I was defiantly not trying to go to a private high school. So I just tried to not pay attention to the kid that was bullying me. It was hard I use to go home and cry so much. I told my parents that I might fight this kid at school.

My parents told me to not to do it, and reminded me about private high school. One day going to school the kid said something about my mom, I was so mad but I did not hit the kid, all I did was yell at him saying stop messing with me, and you better never say anything about my mom because you do not know her. I could get really mad quick when I was young.

A lot of my anger had to do from others making me mad. For example, people lying to me, or that I was not wanted from my real parents and other families not wanting me. I was mad and did not forgive anyone. I had anger in me for so long.

Middle School Love

So when I was at the private middle school, I never really talked to anybody. I had couple friends that was cool, and we did everything together in school. One day I had a feeling inside me, when I saw this girl come down the hallway. I never saw her in the school, because we had different classes. I told my friend aye who is that. He was like that is Annie. I was like aye I want to talk to her.

Mind you at the time, I never went up to a girl before in my life, and I am only in the 7th grade when I saw her. I was too scared to go up to her, so I would just smile a lot when I passed her by. I never talked to the father who adopted me about females, because it never came up. In addition, I was still not fully comfortable talking to them about everything. See at this moment, if kids do not have a father in their life, they will never fully understand how to talk to a female. This is one reason why most dudes in this generation talk to females with no respect, because they never were taught how to talk to a female from their fathers.

That is why I think it is key for a father to be in a child's life, because he can teach the kid some great life lessons. However, because I did not talk to the father who adopted me about females, I went through a whole year without not talking to Annie.

Then, 8th grade came up, and I told myself that I do not need to ask someone on how to talk to a female I got this. One day I went up to Annie and said hi my name is Brayden. She then said back hi, and said I seen you around the school, and she said I seen you few times too. The conversation was going well, and then we had to go back to are classes.

I told myself in my mind that I will like to be her boyfriend. I knew it was a dance coming up at my school, so I was going to ask her to dance with me at the dance. I was so nervous but I went up to her and we danced together I was so happy. After the dance, I went home feeling great, but I still was not her boyfriend. I could not find a perfect way to ask her. This was the downfall of not talking to my father about girls.

I ended up not being her boyfriend, because I waited too long, close to the end of the year she had gotten a boyfriend, and she was moving to another state. I felt a pain inside that I never felt before. I liked her, but did not know how to show it.

The Love Triangle

So after going through not getting Annie in middle school I went in to high school just focus on sports. I made myself so busy with sports I had no time for females, so I thought I could just not think about how to talk to females. Many of my friends had girlfriends and I was single, and was doing me. I sometimes had thoughts of what if I had a girlfriend, but it always went away quick.

What I did not know the more I got older, the more I wanted to talk to females. Therefore, I was in the 12th grade and thought to myself like I need a girlfriend. I was around of many of the popular kids, because I was on the football team, and I knew a lot of people. I still did not know how to talk to females or treat them. I started to look around and copy what the friends I had at the time did. They had many different girls they was talking to, and I was like I want to be like them.

So one day I saw this girl that was pretty tall, and I was like I am going to talk to her. We started to talk and clicked. I was texting her every day after school. Her name was Brittany, and she was in the 11th grade. I then told myself that if my other friends had many girls then I do too. Therefore, I found this girl name Zahura in the 9th grade, that ran track, and I liked that because I played sports. Then I was like this not enough I needed at least three. So one day at my 12th grade homecoming dance this girl name Shaunice from Virginia come down, and I just had to get her, because she was very beautiful.

I had three girls that I was texting and trying to be all their boyfriends. I did not know at the time this was wrong. I thought I was Mr. Big time with three girl's numbers. I now know all I was trying to do was be cool. If I actually talked to my father, he would had sat me down and told me that this is not right. I soon to find out this could not work, because first off I still did not know how to respect females, Brittany and me was always fighting, and having text wars. Then, prom came along I asked Shaunice out to the dance she said yes, but then I forgot that I was actually dating Zahura at the time and I was in a stuck. She was really a good friend that I did not want to hurt, but then Zahura was my girlfriend.

I thought long a hard and I had to blow off Shaunice, and take Zahura to the dance, Shaunice was such a great friend to me so she did not mind. I did not know at the time I did Shaunice so wrong, I almost messed up are friendship. Talking to three girls at the same time was so much work. I told myself after that I would never do it again. Then, with me doing all these bad things I came out of it being single, with Zahura breaking up with me months before prom.

Confusion

In high school, I was going through a lot at the time. I would observe the students and see what they were doing, and I was seeing that most was pregnant or most dudes were just having sex with many girls at once. I was confused on why this was happening. Many of my friends asked me why I was still a virgin, and from that day forward I started to think more and more about having sex.

Then, came one day I was just carving to have sex, and I told this girl to come over, when we was just about to do it she said please don't do this. In my head, I was still trying to have sex, but she did not want to do it. I cannot lie I was mad, but I respected what she wanted. So a year went by and I graduated high school, and I still did not have sex but I would always think about it. I told myself that I need to have sex within this month.

I know this does not sound great, but it was on my mind and I was not going to let anyone stop me. I saw this girl in my college class that was very cute, so I started to flirt with her in class. Weeks went by and I was still flirting with her, then one day we was walking to class and I asked her hey lets skip class. One of the biggest mistakes of my life, but we went to my car, and I told her lets have sex. So we started to have it in my car, after we got done at the moment I was like that's how it feels to have sex.

I went back home that day and was like I need more of that. I called her that night and was like we need to have sex again next week and we did. After having sex with her, I had sex with a two other females. I was reading a book by Nelson Bowen called "A Father's Love or The Lack Thereof" and I learn that the only reason I was trying to have sex with many females was to fill my love tank. Because when I was a child many people abandoned me, I was trying to get the love I did not get from those people who abandoned me from the females.

I know now it was so wrong for me to do that, because I know I might have scared those females for life. They did not know I was doing that; all in their minds was that I was just giving the same love they were giving out.

Great break up

When I was in college, I did not know that I had a problem. My love tank was so low, I was trying to find someone to come into my life and fill it up. I was looking soo hard around my college to find that one girl who is perfect for me. I could not find her, but I did find this one girl name Asia, up the road from me. She went to a different college then me. We started to just text and become friends. I believe after a year went by I decided to take her out to a baseball game for a date.

My heart was beating so fast on this date, because I wanted to make it perfect. I told myself this be the day I ask her if she be my girlfriend. I was so nervous that I sat on ketchup and it was all on my pants, and she and I started to laugh. I think that was like the icebreaker, and we started to have fun.

After that day, she and I was boyfriend and girlfriend, and I went to see her like every week or so. It was hard to see her every day or every week because she lived pretty far, and we were college students so busy. The relationship was still going smooth, because we would text and call each other almost every day. Then when we did go out on dates we would take advantage of the time we got.

Then, 6 months went by and I started to think about sex again, and wonder why her and me did not have any yet. I asked her one day and she told me she was waiting for marriage, so I respected her wishes. I still had sex on my mind, because the love she was giving me was not enough in my mind. I started to listen to others, when they were like she cheating on you. After a year went by and I was still not getting sex with her I started to really think she was cheating on me.

I then did something that I am not proud of doing and I called her and told her we are done. She asked why and I did not want to tell her the true reason why. In my mind, I needed to get more love from her to fill my tank and when I was not getting that I just let her go. I know she was hurting, and I had to face the fact that I hurt another female for all the wrong reasons. It seemed I could never have a healthy relationship.

Word Up

During my time in college, I had many problems that I wanted to fix. I really did not know where to go, or how to fix them I was truly lost. One day I was eating with some friends in the café, and this random girl came to my table and asks my friends and me if we wanted to attend her bible study on the campus. I told her yea I come, but in my mind, I was like this going to be lame. I walked in the room and I saw some people I knew and I was like what's good.

I stayed for the whole thing, because my friends were in there. The teacher that was teaching the bible study lesson that day was Dr. Lindsay. I really do not remember the lesson, but I know I felt a great vibe from her, felt welcome. She went around the room asking us questions, to get us feeling that we are wanted. I even felt something inside me that she asked me about my childhood and I told the whole room about it, which I do not just tell everyone. However, something inside me felt like I should share it.

It felt so great to be able to share part of my childhood. It was scary to me that this bible study got me to open up. They said that the bible study was called Word Up and it is always on Wednesdays. I went back the next week and I had a good time, but then some of my friends did not want to go back so the following week I did not go because I was following what others thought. I knew inside that the bible study was going to get me back with God, and fix my problems. I did not go back to the bible study for a whole semester.

Then, I learned that most of my mistakes was from being around people who I thought was my friends, but truly was not. They was not on the path I was trying to go, so I had to leave them behind, and once I did that I started to go back to more of the bible studies.

By me going to these bible studies, I started to make friends that wanted the best for me and pushed me to get there. I started to fellowship and have great times with my new friends. I even found a new church, because of the bible study, which I rededicated my life back to God. Doing this some of my problems God fixed for me.

iNgage

I told you how I was in a bible study called Word Up. I then keep on telling myself I needed to do something bigger. I started to write in a journal, and I told myself I wanted to help change this generation. I was so sick of seeing how the world was becoming, but I would not lie I did not know where to start. So for a whole year I just keep on thinking and writing.

Then, one day a friend name Rhema called me and asked me if I wanted to come to this community day thing. I was like yea it was during summer time too, so I thought I would be getting free food plus the event was free too. I went that day, and I had a great time. The event surprised me, because it was fun and unique. What really hit it off was a young man named Nelson was on the stage preaching a lesson, and I felt like I needed to get to know more of him. I even brought one of his books, and he signed it.

After that day I told myself this might be the thing that I can do that is so much bigger. Plus I wanted to be a part of this, because I felt it will do great things. I keep on going to the worship experiences, and then that one-day Nelson asks if I would like to volunteer and be a greater. I was so happy, because I was ready to do anything for iNgage. I came to volunteer each worship experience and never missed a day. I loved to help and I tried to do everything. I really loved iNgage, because one day Nelson told everyone that the mission for iNgage was "To see a generation healed and city changed through the HOPE of Jesus Christ". I was so happy to hear that, because a year ago I wanted to see a generation healed, and now I get to do it with a great team.

Being a part of INgage is such a blessing and they treat me just like family I love it. In addition, I relate so much to Nelson, because we kinda went through the same childhood, and in his book and him talking to me helped me understand and learn a lot. I learned so much from him, and I am so thankful for that. Also, being part of INgage helped me grow more and stretched me, because they put me in charge of things that I am not great at, but they have trusted me and know I will do great.

21 and Going

I am now 21 making this book and I am still trying to find my birth parents. I will not lie to you it is very hard to not be sad that I still do not know my parents or even my other brother and sister. I try to think of positive things when I get sad. For example, the type of environment I was in as a child was not suitable for me. I would be around a lot of bad influences. Then, I would not have the opportunity to meet the great parents I have now.

The parents I am with will never understand how I feel inside, but they will always try to love me and show that they are here for me. I love that and appreciate it to the fullest. As a child that is in the same situation as I am in, I want to see yall think about the positive things that comes from being an adopted. God wants you to be happy and he giving you another home is showing that he loves you and wants the best. Stay strong and keep on praying if you are looking for your parents, and if God has it in your life to meet back with your parents he will make it happen.

It is very easy to say this to yall, than act it out in life. I will tell you it has been nights when I would think about my birth parents, and cry and cry. I know your pain I would get in arguments for no reason, just because I am mad that I have not seen my birth parents. Do not do what I have done, and be better than I am. Control your anger, pray to God, and he will make you at pace.

Thanks You's

Shaunice thanks for always caring even though I cancelled on you at the last minute for my prom.

Brittany thanks for being real even though I use to treat you like a jerk in high school.

Annie thanks for being so nice to me even though I did not know how to show my emotions.

Zahura thanks for being so nice to me even though I was not giving it back.

I want to give thanks to some of the friends I had when I was young, yall really helped me out so I could feel wanted.

India thanks for inviting me to Word Up, and helping me become a better person.

Dr. Linsday and G thanks for really helping me redicating my life back to God. Yall helped so much and still are thanks and love yall.

My word up family thanks for helping me too, because yall made my family even bigger, and made me feel special.

Deveraux thanks for being you, because you always do great things and that pushes me sometimes to work harder, and do even greater things good look son.

INgage family thanks so much for being in my life, I love all yall so much, I cannot wait to keep fighting beside yall. We will see a generation healed, and a city changed, through the HOPE of Jesus Christ.

Jeff thanks for being someone I could talk to and really get deep with. I am thankful God put you in my life, and thanks for praying on me.

Nelson thanks for being another great person that been there for me, because of you I learned so much of how to be a better man. We are going to take this city by storm and nothing will stop us. Also, thanks for making your book it helped me a lot these past months and I used some information in your book, for my book. You making that book really changed me for the better, and made me a better man. Love you man.

Garrett and Julie Dyer (Mom and Dad) thanks so much for everything. It is so much you did for me and still are doing for me. I am so thankful for one big thing you did for me, that is making me a Dyer. Love you.

Also, I want to give thanks to other people that I might did not say, but remember you do great things in this world not to get recognized, but you do it because it is the right thing to do, and you want to do it.

God I love you so much thank you so much for putting some great parents in my life and giving me the best life I could possible live. Thank so much I get to live in your creation and do it not having to worry about big problems. I love you always and never will stop.

Made in the USA
Middletown, DE
04 January 2024

46910736R00017